Mommy Works,
Daddy Works

170301

by Marika Pedersen and Mikele Hall

illustrations by Deirdre Betteridge

Annick Press Ltd.   Toronto • New York • Vancouver

Kendra •• Jason • Sean
... If it
weren't for
you, we would not
be working
mommies.
Terran •• Kiana

—M.P. and M.H.

For my grandma.
All my love
—D.B.

We acknowledge the support of the Canada Council for the Arts, the Ontario Arts Council, and the Government of Canada through the Book Publishing Industry Development Program (BPIDP) for our publishing activities.

Cataloging in Publication Data

Pedersen, Marika
    Mommy works, Daddy works

ISBN 1-55037-657-8 (bound)   ISBN 1-55037-656-X (pbk.)

1. Occupations – Juvenile literature. I. Hall, Mikele. II. Betteridge, Deirdre. III. Title.

HF5381.2.P42 2000   j331.7'02   C00-930585-8

The art in this book was rendered in mixed media.
The text was typeset in Smile.

Distributed in Canada by:
Firefly Books Ltd.
3680 Victoria Park Avenue
Willowdale, ON
M2H 3K1

Published in the U.S.A. by Annick Press (U.S.) Ltd.
Distributed in the U.S.A. by:
Firefly Books (U.S.) Inc.
P.O. Box 1338
Ellicott Station
Buffalo, NY 14205

Printed and bound in Canada by Friesens, Altona, Manitoba.

visit us at: **www.annickpress.com**

My daddy rollerblades to work.
My daddy is a dance teacher.
He shows people how to move their
bodies to music and become stronger.

But there is always time for me!

My mommy works from home.
My mommy is a writer.
She writes books from her office
upstairs for people to buy and read.

But there is always time for me!

My mommy goes to work.

My mommy takes the bus to work.
My mommy is a police officer.
Her police car has lights and
a siren to let people know that
she is there to help.

What does your mommy do?

My daddy goes to work.

My daddy rides a motorcycle to work.
My daddy is a construction worker.
He helps people build places to
work and places to play.

What does your daddy do?

My daddy stays home.
My daddy is a homemaker.
My daddy's job is to look after me
and take care of the work that
needs to be done around the house.

But there is always time for me!

My mommy takes the train downtown. She is the president of a company and makes sure everything runs smoothly.

But there is always time for me!

My daddy walks to work.
My daddy is a chef.
He cooks weird-looking meals
that people love to eat.
I like his desserts the best.

But there is always time for me!

My mommy rides a bike to work.
My mommy is a letter carrier.
She delivers cards, packages and magazines
to people who are waiting for them.

But there is always time for me!

My daddy rides a subway to work.
My daddy is an architect.
He designs buildings and skyscrapers.

But there is always time for me!

My mommy stays home.
My mommy is a homemaker.
My mommy's job is to look after me
and take care of the work that
needs to be done around the house.

But there is always time for me!

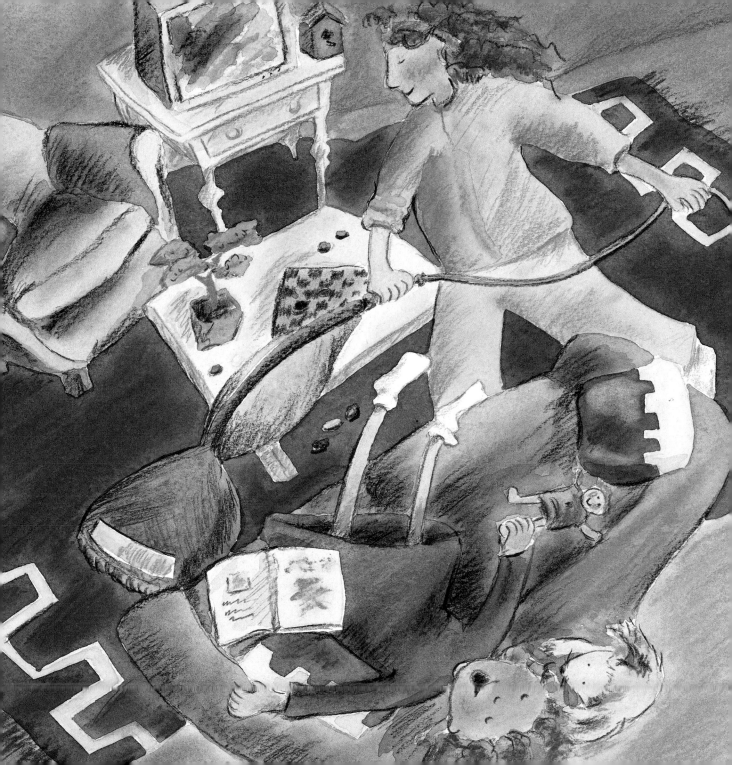

My daddy works from home.
He is a famous musician.
He practices the trumpet in
the attic and sometimes teaches
other people to play.

But there is always time for me!

My mommy drives to work.
My mommy is a pilot.
She flies people to countries all
over the world so they can go
on holiday or on business trips.

But there is always time for me!

My daddy rides a tractor for work.
My daddy is a farmer.
He plows fields and sows seeds to grow
food for people to buy and then to eat.

But there is always time for me!

My mommy carpools to work.
My mommy is a salesperson.
She sells computers to other
mommies and daddies.

But there is always time for me!

My daddy drives to work.
My daddy is a bus driver.
He helps busy people get
from place to place.

But there is always time for me!

My mommy jogs to work.
My mommy is a fitness instructor.
She teaches people to exercise and
take care of their bodies.

But there is always time for me!

It doesn't matter how busy my mommy is, she always has time to give me kisses and hugs.

It doesn't matter how much work my daddy has, because at the end of the day he always gives me kisses and hugs.